nostalgia

nostalgia

nostalgia

brin battisti

nostalgia

Cover Image: Unknown

Section Images: Pinterest stock images

ISBN: 9781078368537

**this is for all of those
who believe they'll be stuck
forever in the past
you'll make it out**

nostalgia

warning:

this book touches upon sensitive topics such as

emotional abuse

depression

dealing with trauma

self-harm

and other possible triggers

please remember to take care of yourselves
always

nostalgia

table of contents

nostalgia

lost & bleeding

nostalgia

my story,

it was never pretty

it was never poetic

and it certainly

never meant to end up here in your hands

but i'm learning that sometimes

the only way to move forward

is to leave it on the pages

sometimes writing it all down can grant a form of
closure

no person could ever give you

i had never felt more afraid

i was alone
lost somewhere in the middle of my journey
beaten, bruised, and bleeding

the only thing i seemed to be able to do
to escape my emotions and situation
was curl up in a ball, hidden
and reminisce of better times

-when the ghosts first started coming

nostalgia

some days

that sick feeling deep

in the pit of my stomach

is more prominent

than other days

it's the regret i hold inside me

its poisonous roots spreading

blackening my veins until

the blood looks like ink

that sick feeling is what

holds me back most days

when i try to take

a new step forward

just feed me some
pretty little lies
leave the evidence laying around

let me figure the rest out on my own

and soon all that's healed is
open and bleeding again

-a guide on how to b r e a k me

nostalgia

the year end

is always the worst

because it's so full of

endings and darkness and

cold and fear of all changes

i can't help but think of all the

things i have done this year

(and all those other years)

and i just feel as though

i gain so very much

at the beginning

but by the end

i lose it all

again

(i hope it's true when they say it's always darkest before dawn)

the lies were the worst part of it all

i remember him telling me

everything from you was a lie

*you never loved me, i was never enough and never would
have been enough for you*

so why did you let me feel like i could be?

he is literally pleading with me as

i am sobbing so hard my chest hurts and i want to throw
up and the only thing racing through my mind is

why are you blaming me for how you *made* me *feel, why
are you telling me all this*

*when you are burdening your angry mind and your
stupid lies onto me,* when you knew

i *was the one that was never enough*

when i *was the one that you never really loved*

-*displacement*

nostalgia

winter is suffocating to me

the crushing cold

wrapping her fingers around me

making my body numb

my breath catching in my chest

the dirty slush getting all over

my white boots

this heavy blanket of snow and

nostalgia trying to

bury me

it's kind of

exactly how you made me feel

when you squished my entire being

down into the dirt with your foot

-overpowered

denial

i just cannot accept that you have left

the bed where you used to lie
colder than ice
a hole ripped in my chest
where my heart used to be
i still talk like you're here
when everyone knows you aren't
i still feel your iron grip pinning me to the ground
still hear your voice,
all your lies, accusations, reminders, and anger
running circles in my head
i still see your ghost
around every corner

and honestly,
i guess i enjoy the company your ghost gives me

-five stages of grief

nostalgia

i watch your teeth
sink into the gooey black middle of an apple
that looked perfectly pristine
when you picked it up

and when you bite into the ugly rot
while it drips down your chin

you don't even seem surprised
that the inside is rotten

and that's when i realized
the way you chose to break me

each stab was intended

-nightmare

you know that feeling
when you're trying to sleep
and you sit up and glance at your clock
and the red lights read back
12:29 a.m.
and you realize

you're in for a long night

nostalgia

the things my ghosts whisper to me

are a million times scarier

than the ghosts that yell *boo!*

and then disappear

-i don't like this haunting

how am i supposed to let them go?

how can i get them back?

what could i have done different to make them stay?

is it possible to change their mind?

why does everyone end up leaving?

-google search

nostalgia

the problem with fairy tales is

they portray midnight

as a whimsical

magical time where destinies fall

into place

they don't tell you that in real life

it's where you'll fall apart

if you're still awake

-midnight needs a disclaimer

i'd used to cling to you
like frost would cling
to the windshield of my car
in the early winter mornings

i'd always thought that
maybe
you could save me from
my own mind

and you did, for some time
i thought of you at night
instead of my mistakes
but then
all the things you said were my fault
started coming to me at night

and i don't know what was worse
my past mistakes haunting me
or the torture all those fights
was putting me through

nostalgia

she *used* to believe in happy endings
and fairy tales
    and magic
        and light

he *used* to believe in heroes
and epic quests
    and that the good guys
        always win

then look at those kids now
with a heavy heart
knowing their innocence will be
the one thing they wish
they still had

because growing older
means facing the real world

and one can only stay ignorant
for so long

how to be happy

how to move on

how to let it all go

how to stop thinking so much

how to stop caring so much

-google search pt. II

nostalgia

i think the last of my innocence was gone
when i felt like i stopped seeing things in color
that's when i knew something was wrong with me
and even then
i didn't want help

it took almost losing everything
it took seeing each day as black and grey and
my skin as a pale white sickly smear in the mirror
to fully grasp what i was truly doing
to everyone around me

it wasn't just me that i stopped seeing in color
it was leaking onto the pallets of others too
and i my sadness
caused everyone around me to go monotone too
because of how sensitive and fragile i was
like a dead flower that crumbled at someone's touch

i thought i would never see the color of a sunflower ever
again

brin battisti

i don't think

black

and white

and grey

and monochrome sadness

are my colors

-i don't like looking like sadness

nostalgia

i flew through the first thirteen years

of my lifelong journey

but it would appear that

the second i made it into middle school

i hit a rock wall

a tornado came and

knocked me off my path

and for the next five years

i just wander aimlessly

the thing is, i can see my path clearly

but for some reason

these vines tangled around my torso

seem much more comforting

much more inviting

than the fear

of the unknown

i cannot seem
to get out of my own
head but i am also
out of my mind

i don't *want* to grow up
> i don't *want* to get older
>> i don't *want* to lose this feeling

i have no desire to change

i feel like the past has a tight grip on me
ropes made of memories
binding my wrists together

pulling me away from moving on
and i'm too *scared*
to cut them

i wish i weren't so scared

scared of my own mind

and the dark

and of falling asleep

and of being alone

i wish i could just function

presently

as any other human can

the most important part

of moving forward

with your life

is the part where

you stop

clinging to the past

like it

still

means

something

-it doesn't

nostalgia

they always ask

if they still have a part of me

even when they have

been gone for ages

i'm too scared to tell them

that in my writing

they'll always live on

so i just say no

and continue to create their stories

on my own time

brin battisti

all these ghosts around me

it doesn't make for
any good conversation

nostalgia

i've become addicted

to the relief and the pain

i can feel

when i write you down on these pages

even though you're long gone

why is it such a chore
for me to let go?

there is no way
to go back
so why can't i
move forward

-regression

nostalgia

people like you
are the reason i cower in fear
and allow myself to be thrown against a brick wall
over and over again

because i would rather be the one
getting hurt
than seeing people like *you* hurt

people like you
are the reason i wrap my arms
around my core though i don't know
if i'm trying to warm or protect myself
because people like you
leave me damaged and frozen inside

i can't help but think

about how our story

went

so bad

so fast

and i feel like that just

exposed

layers upon layers

of

b l a c k

v i l e

r o t

underneath a beautiful flower bed

built to cover and hide

what we already knew

was there in the first place

-i guess we were just poison to each other

nostalgia

every snowflake that falls this winter

will simply be another memory

falling from the sky

onto my bare skin

and then melting away

for some reason

i still try to cling to the

sensation of cold

the burning flakes leave

even after the snow stopped falling

days ago

the beginnings
are never the hard part
and that is probably
what haunts me the most

in the beginning we create such beauty
create the most amazing story
only for it to crash and burn then die out
as the year comes to a close

the ashes of our story strewn across
the field of pure white snow
a giant hole sixty feet deep where our asteroid
made impact

-*why do the good things always end so bad?*

nostalgia

i'm lost

alone

scared

and dying

on the forest floor and

all around me i just see the eyes

of people surrounding me and

watching me bleed out

entertained by my pain

with no sense of sympathy

and no reason to reach out and

help me

the saddest part of it all

is that they are all people

i reached out to and i helped

when they were where i am now

it's the sense of impending doom

that gets to me

these late winter nights

like for some reason

the end of the year also means

the end of everything i've known

almost as if the world is going to be destroyed

once the clock hits twelve

on december 31st

nostalgia

i'd like to think that maybe

we could have worked together

that despite all of the signs

telling us

we were just not meant to be

that we could have beaten the odds

but i'd be lying if i said

i didn't know that it just wasn't

written in the cards

for you and i to last together

it was only a matter of time

before one of us crumbled

at the hands of the other

brin battisti

do you hate me now
after the dust has settled and
we are no longer a part of each other's lives
do you still think and worry about me
the way i do

or do you regret ever meeting me
are you wishing you never hit send
that day our world's first collided

-was i a mistake?

nostalgia

she wraps her burning hot

inky tendrils

around my brain

and squeezes

as hard as she can

-paranoia

the little girl i used to be

never could have wrapped her carefree mind

around how suffocating

growing older gets to be

she would have never imagined

never being able to breathe

because the disgusting vision that she's forced to live

has an iron grip around her lungs

she would never have pictured

not being able to stand

because everyone else forced her to

place a bulletproof cage around her heart

she would have never understood

what it's like to be silenced

because she was told that as a teenager and as a woman

what she had to say didn't matter

duct tape placed over her lips

nostalgia

i still have so much to say

there is too much left to release

still too much blame

being placed on me and only me

i still have so many suppressed

thoughts

hidden emotions

things i knew i could never say to you

because it would still end up being my fault

and all of it is still raging and swirling

inside of me

but it will never be said because

we ended so abruptly

-what do i do with all these unsaid words?

i know

if you're ever reading this

you're going to be angry with me

not only for writing about you

but for including it here

and for making you

seem so bad

but

this is the only way

i know how to cope with it all

and this is the only way

i'll ever get the past

out of my head and honestly

to me, it was that bad

and so

i need it on these papers instead

nostalgia

i don't know

if magic is real anymore

or if it ever even really existed

in the first place

but if it is

can someone please

point me in the direction

of a person who can just

send me back?

why did you give up on me

when i never once

gave up on you?

why did you blame me for everything

when we were both

guilty parties?

why was it always my wrongdoing

when you never saw

how broken your words made me?

why couldn't you just see me?

did you not like what you saw?

this is a terrible war

i've got raging inside me

to be so terrified of change

but to need it so desperately as well

to know that our entire world

needs to change or we will all die

but to be so afraid to live and grow

to avoid the future and try surviving in the past

i know that i must live my life

i must blossom

i must carry on

but i have no desire to do so

because i don't want to lose

what i have with me

right now

you used to feel like home to me

your smile was like daybreak

your laughter was music

your embrace just flooded me with warmth

leaving me feeling safe and secure

how tragic is it

that my home was ripped to shreds in

less than a day

wood rotting and

cobwebs and dirt already in all of the cracks and corners

i guess our foundation was already weak

because of how fast it all crumbled into

dust

nostalgia

last time i was sitting here

i was daydreaming about you

writing your full name across this paper

thinking about how when i got home

i'd be texting you

facetiming you

maybe i'd even be getting ready to go over to your house

a year later

and i'm sitting in this same exact chair

staring at that same clock

in between those same windows

writing this poem

brin battisti

just let me go

my younger self begs me

i can't

i weep back

nostalgia

what would you say to the you from a year ago?

someone asked me

and i kind of laugh a little

oh there's a whole list of things

i said

like what?

like

listen to your friends. you need to leave him. he is only toxic, he is manipulative, he is immature, he is only hurting you. listen. because what they are telling you is right, and he only hurt you in the end. but the damage done was too great.

now, you apologize for things out of your control, things that aren't your fault, things that you didn't do. you worry endlessly that every word out of your mouth will trigger an argument. you don't sleep at night. anything will spike your anxiety, cause a panic attack. you worry he still watches you.

like

stand up for yourself, let your she-wolf out, let her play,
let her howl as loud as she can. because now, she is
silent. now she is buried. now she can't say no, can't
defend her beliefs, can't tell someone else they are in the
wrong, can't tell someone she's upset. now, she's
snuffed out, the fire in her belly is gone.

like

take your own advice, or else you're going to end up
long forgotten. used and thrown to the side like no one
wants you, no one needs you. because that's what
happens doll. you never know who you can trust, and
you trust too easily, too fast, and you get thrown face
down in the dirt.

like

don't let the little things bother you

i end up saying instead

nostalgia

living with you in my life

was like living

locked and shackled to the ground

in the farthest corner of a dirty cellar

the only times i was granted freedom

would be for me to do

what was necessary

for any basic human need

to be given food

to shower

and to be visited by you

any contact with other people

or with the outside world

was forbidden

social media was not allowed,

the only reason i even had access to a phone

was for me to talk to you and only you

whenever i was able to break free

for even a few split

glorious seconds before you found me

i was actually alive

living and free

i experienced more of the world in those stolen seconds

than i ever did in those ten

solitary, lonely months with you

all i ever wanted was some form of freedom

to be able to have some time

to myself

to not be treated like a child

to be allowed friends and time out

and now that you're gone i can't leave this

ugly grey basement because you forgot to leave the keys

forgot to unlock these chains

forgot to cut the puppet strings loose

nostalgia

winter wrapped her cold
icy hands
around my waist and pulled
her grasp around me iron

she said
isn't it just so easy
to stay here in the dark
and relieve each and every torturous moment

isn't it so easy to curl up and try to hide
from the past that my mind and soul is trapped in
she told me she will always here
she'll hand me any memory i ask for
feed them into my mind and engrave them herself
she said she isn't afraid to play the hard things
she isn't scared to take me down and bury my body
under mountains of heavy wet snow
and

she said at least here

living back then

instead of right now

i'll already know the outcomes

of trying to take risks

and random bursts of spontaneous courage

and so i take her hand

and try to find some form of solace

if i can't find comfort

in her freezing fingertips

-why am i so afraid to let go?

nostalgia

how do i beat all the odds stacked against me

and move on?

how am i supposed to let go when everything i do

i just get reminded of my mistakes?

how do i forgive myself?

-google search pt III

as this year ends and

the new one is bound to begin

i can only think back on what i went through this year

and how much changed

and i realize

that losing you

may have been one of the best things that could have
happened to me

because i've never felt more free

than i do now, here in this moment without you by my
side

i will never regret being with you

because there were good memories and good times

but you also taught me a lot

you helped me learn how i should be treated

and that what we had wasn't healthy or okay

and now that i have this

i no longer need closure

nostalgia

i may never get over some events

or certain people

the memories attached

are too traumatic

to just let go

i may still be scared to trust

or worry too much

and ask questions obsessively

to ensure

that i won't cause people to leave me

and to make sure

i am not too much for you

but still

i think i can finally see

the beginning of daybreak

brin battisti

the darkness of both

this past winter

and this night

being broken up by rays of light

and i can finally understand why they say

it's always darkest before dawn

nostalgia

it's time to let go of my old friends

time to tell winter she needs to go

time to find my path and

actually begin my journey again

time to patch up my wounds

time to tell fear she must release me from these shackles

and it's time for me

to let the past float away from my spirit

and because i know this and want to begin to change

i begin to walk towards the warm light

with flower buds laced through my hair

the damage done to my soul no longer bleeding heavily

my bare feet stepping from the slush into grass

the howling wind transforming to a light breeze

and for just a few moments at least

i feel like my soul was flying

brin battisti

Henn Kim

band aids
&
battle cries

nostalgia

i'm only halfway through

the biggest battle of

my lifetime

the one where i with either

forgive myself for

all the pain i put me through

or i fall

-*civil war*

it is an awful habit of mine

the way i cover up all my

broken parts

cuts and fear

with band-aids

when really i need

stitches

i need casts and i need anything

stronger than a band-aid

-i need to stop being ignorant

nostalgia

i unfortunately still wake

to missing you

i still reach out for you in the early mornings

my fingertips stretched out

as far as they can go

but i've also come to learn

you won't ever be there

and that it really is just

all for the better

brin battisti

all in due time my dear
spring tells me
when i ask her why
i cannot yet unshackle myself
since spring is supposed to be
a new start
rebirth and
a fresh beginning

you are still learning to walk
and until you know how
you can't yet walk away
from what troubles you

nostalgia

anger

all i feel towards you right now is anger

i'm angry with you for holding me back

for preventing me from living

for keeping me locked away like

you owned me and i was an animal

you had to keep caged up

not only that

but for blaming me, for the fact that you were always the
victim

i'm angry at your refusal to see other sides

and refusal to listen when everyone was explaining to
you, you're wrong

i'm angry i was always to blame

and i'm angry you tricked me into falling for it

-five stages of grief pt. II

brin battisti

the way i lost you

wasn't poetic

but

i

write

it

into

poetry

anyway

-coping mechanisms

nostalgia

the little girl i used to be

just wants some peace of mind

-*yet i can't let her have it*

brin battisti

i don't know how it's possible for someone
to go from love to hate
in a matter of only a few seconds
but i saw it happen

and i can only start to feel
as though the love
was never really there
in the first place

and that was the very beginning
of all the lies you fed me

nostalgia

when you are with someone
it's meant to be sweet
and warm
loving and open and soft
but somehow indestructible too

i never expected i would be so afraid and scared
that you would cut me with the
jagged sharp edges of what you told me
was your care and feelings and emotions
you felt towards me

i never expected to be shaking and crying
hiding on the floor of my room
the lights off
door locked
protected by someone else until i could go home

maybe i should have seen the warning signs

i saw you the other day

and i noticed you were wearing

the hoodie i bought you for your birthday

and i began to wonder

were you ever able to wash my scent

out of your clothes?

the perfume i would always wear

because you said it was your favorite one

or do you still smell me faintly

every time you wear the clothes i always stole from you

because i still smell you on my skin

and no amount of soap

is going to get rid of it

nostalgia

i never thought i would be someone

to hang on to the past

considering i forgive so easily

and i've always been willing to move on from

the mistakes people had made

but as i grow up and

as people had begun taking advantage of my forgiveness

and as forgiving turned into turning a blind eye

to the way i was being treated

i began holding on

i start looking for any reason why i should stay

even if it is a reason as simple as

we had a good day today

amongst a sea of endless bad days

i'd cling to that good day and

i'd blindly, naïvely stay

grasping at any straw i could find to tell myself that

they are just out of it

it'll get better soon

because the truth is

it didn't get better

it got worse

and all i could do was

look away and hold on tightly to that one time

six months ago

when we were happy for a few hours

my biggest strength

and my biggest weakness

is my ability to choose to only see good in people

it often times kills me

it leaves me bleeding on the floor with my heart on the ground next to me and yet still

i can't help it

i have this undying hope that these people won't treat me and abuse me and use me the same way

those people did

i couldn't help it

until you came

and you showed me no amount of optimism and sacrifice and trust and hope

was ever going to mask the person you were

and i believe that was the day my little sunray went out

your ghost came to visit again

you told me no one is ever going to love me

for whom i am

and that for you personally,

it was all a lie

it was fake

i think it's time for you to go now

i tell your ghost

standing up rapidly, knocking my drink down the front
of my shirt

my voice trembling with tears falling down my cheeks

and with one

perfectly evil grin

you make your exit

-but i know you'll be back

nostalgia

you smile at me

coax me to you

bribing me with promises of

safety and rescue

stupidly i go

and just like i had always done

you hand me band-aids

to cover the knife wounds

you put on my soul

no, nothing was physical but

the mental toll was enough to leave

my spirit crippled

and still, i reached out and took the band-aid

from your hand anyway

-band-aids can't heal everything

brin battisti

for a split second

the dust clears

the bombs stop falling

the fighting inside me

stops

for that split second

i get a brief taste

and a slight glimpse

of what lays on the other side

of this battlefield

of mine

-ceasefire

nostalgia

as i watch this

new spring blossom

i can't help but

be jealous

of all those new flowers

that get to bloom

a fresh new start

a reset

to their year

they get to grow and sprout

after being dormant since the previous year

and each time they grow

they are more beautiful

i want a chance

to become that beautiful too

instead of being the girl with

no color in her face and

those sad eyes

brin battisti

i want the chance to be able

to grow again

all brand-new

without any of this weight

i can't imagine

the things i would be able to do

if i were given the chance

to forget all the bad

-i wish i had a reset button

nostalgia

it's strange to me

how even if it's been years

since i last saw you

i'll still be sad

looking at your pictures

and wondering

what happened to the person

i once knew so well

brin battisti

what you do know:

was that you leaving

left me bleeding

what you don't know:

it wasn't blood

coming from the wounds

you inflicted

it was ink

ink and words began pouring

from the open cuts

and taking the pen in my hand

and writing it down

was how i began to heal

that first night without you

all i was able to do was

cry

      cry

          cry

             cry

                cry

-letting you go

brin battisti

that second night without you

all i was able to do was

                    think

              think

         think

     think

think

-letting you go II

nostalgia

that third night without you

all i was able to do was

wonder

      wonder

          wonder

              wonder

                  (what did i do wrong?)

-letting you go III

that fourth night without you
all i was able to do was

                        write

                write

          write

     write

write

-i've let you go, i've learned to cope

nostalgia

you told me once that you bet
you never cross my mind
that i don't even think about you
unless you reach out first

that was almost four years ago
and little do you know how often
your ghost frequents the empty spaces of my mind

even though we haven't spoken since my birthday
those four years ago

brin battisti

writing became the gauze

i use to cover up the

emotional mess

you all left me in

and it has become the superglue

i use to

hold all my broken pieces together

nostalgia

imagine what it must be like for

a thirteen-year-old girl

to find more comfort

crying on a bathroom floor

locked away from the rest of the world

tortured by things out of her control but she still

still blames herself anyway

instead of finding comfort in the people that surround
her

because she knows that no one is paying attention

no one notices that she needs help and

no one listens to her when she speaks

so she handles things in

the most toxic way

but the only way she thinks

will help her feel better

-invisible

now imagine that thirteen-year-old

now sixteen and

in therapy and trying to get better

really fighting because now she understands that

the things she was doing really hurt the people around
her

once everyone found out

but they still don't care

this sixteen-year old girl is still invisible

still fighting a battle all on her own

because no one can give her an ounce of care

even though she drops everything she's doing

to help the people she loves the most

so she pushes it down instead

she takes up painting and

a million of different sports to try and occupy her mind

but her demons and ghosts still find her at night

-invisible II

nostalgia

and now this girl is eighteen and she

thinks that she is better, thinks that she is strong

she can laugh and smile and have a good time

but then there are people

the very ones she said *i love you* to and shared her
deepest secrets with

the ones she opened up to about her sadness and
depression and anxiety and fear

and they used it to their advantage

this one forced her to feel guilty and take blame for
wanting to do something for herself

he told her love was about making sacrifices

he locked her away in a basement and told her she has to
be alone with no one but him

and riddled her mind with lies and poison and abuse and
she let it because she thought it was love and she thought
it was only normal because pain, it was all she was used
to

and so she fell again

-invisible III

and now she is nineteen she survived all of it and despite
feeling invisible

she knows what she went through, and she knows she
can only be better because of it...

i still feel invisible sometimes but, moving on with my
life and choosing to work it all out regardless of how
hard it may be to get up some days

has made me who i am today

i look at what others have done to me and i use it as an
example of who i don't want to allow myself to become

i still struggle, i still shut down, i still have horrible days
but

since cutting out the most negative people and removing
myself from negative places

i have grown stronger

i may not be completely healed, or completely moved on
but,

for now, i'm alive and the scars i bear represent my fight

and that must count for something

-maybe i'm not so invisible anymore

nostalgia

maybe

with this new year

i'll try to loosen my grasp

to the past

just a little

each day

instead of gripping it in my fists

with knuckles so white

you could almost see my bone

-a resolution i'm dying to complete

brin battisti

my heart is still

stuck

shaped like the

inside of your fist

from when you squeezed

(a little too hard)

nostalgia

the only person

that can rescue me

is myself and it just seems that

i can't

no

i won't

take the steps i need to take

to get there

and honestly

i have no reason for it

we had some good moments

and in our time spent together

i clung to those memories

and when you left i clung to all the bad

to remind myself that's why you're gone

that's why i should be okay with it

truthfully

i need to stop looking at it as all good

or all bad

it was a mix of it all and i suppose

our emotions were too different in the end

i loved you too much

and you thought i loved you too little

you think you loved me too much

when really

you didn't love me at all

it's time for me to come to terms with this and take the
scissors

and cut the remaining strings you forgot to take with you
when you left

nostalgia

i think

i need to do the hardest part

and rip the band-aid

off of all of my wounds

i need to let them air out

i need to stop focusing on them

i need to let nature do its thing

that'll be the only way

these cuts will heal

i have yet to walk out of this cage

you shoved me in

i keep thinking that

every time i step out

you'll come for me

you'll show up to out the chains back on

and lock me back down to the ground

so for now

i just stand in the doorway

battling with desire and fear

nostalgia

past comes to visit me today

to tell me i won't make something of myself

the way i want to

and to tell me that i will never rid myself of her

she tells me

that i'll be stuck here with her tied right by my side

for the rest of time

that i won't ever be able to live or be free

and for the first time ever

with silver tears streaming down my cheeks

my voice shaking uncontrollably

i tell her

no

i will find a way to destroy you

and i will find a way to fly again without you

-*revolution*

i wipe my tears
i force myself to stand, my legs unstable and
my breathing ragged
but i do it anyway

i force myself to take that first step out of that cage
my heart pounding and
my head spinning
but i do it anyway

and then i walk all the way to the door
the light hitting my face
my eyes squinting in the sudden brightness
the sun shines on me
my thoughts racing

but i do it anyway

-*breakaway*

nostalgia

i take a deep breath

and i step out into the budding spring

the field covered in wildflowers

it's the first time i'm going out

since you chained me in that dark basement

and my hands won't stop shaking, i'm so scared you'll
come for me

but with each step i take

with the cool grass under my bare feet

i feel the nerves fall away

and for the first time in over a year

my mind

just for a bit

is clear of the thought of you

i sit down in the middle of that field

made of wildflowers and spring

sits right next to me

she braids my hair

makes me a crown of

daisies and lilies and daffodils

and she tells me that

my mind can create such beautiful things

if only i let it

-breakaway II

nostalgia

and when i finally

get back on my feet

in the middle of that field

the wildflowers pass me my sword

i adjust my crown

and i have never been

more ready to fight

brin battisti

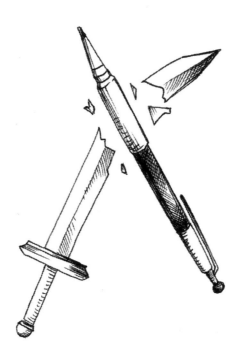

war wounds

&

surrender

nostalgia

in this next battle

i am going to burn my enemies

to the ground

and i am going to ensure

they feel my raging desire

to finish the war that i started

i will bring them to their knees

-surrender

brin battisti

the girl within me
finally succumbs
she waves her white flag

and for the first time
since i was thirteen

i feel hope

-surrender II

bargaining

i would plead, cry, beg, bribe, and do whatever i could
both to you and to myself

i would tell you i'll do whatever it took
to get you back
i said that you just need to tell me
what you need from me to stay
and i'll give it to you

i begged my mind to release you
from her grasp because this was a good thing
and the only thing you were doing to me was
intoxicating me with the deadliest venom
killing me from the inside out
and whatever she needed to forget you
i'd give it to her, because i needed you gone

-five stages of grief III

brin battisti

i start letting my

war wounds show

because how else will everyone know

how i got here

and i will be able to take

whatever they throw at me

nostalgia

when i look at the true meaning

of nostalgia

i realize now i was never

and still am not

feeling nostalgic

i don't miss the past necessarily

and i have spent a lot of my life

running from it

trying to escape all the bad that kept

replaying in my head like I was

re-watching all my favorite shows

i don't know what i would call it

exactly

but it's grip on me is getting looser and

it's burden a little lighter

i still visit some of the places

that were special to us

but now i make my own memories here

i've stopped coming here to grieve

what i thought i lost

and i don't come here

bearing the chains of a prisoner

anymore

instead i visit with

a journal in one hand and

a pen in the other

and i write down my story

(not ours)

the story of a girl who's finally free to

love and do whatever she please

without needing to worry

(too much)

nostalgia

summer is here
and i like the feeling of independence
it brings
with each new day

there are still days

and moments where

i can't stop looking over my shoulder

and i have to do double

no triple checks

because that person that was in the elevator

looked exactly like you

and there are still nights

i lie awake questioning what i did to you

to warrant your actions against me and all the

pointed words and knife-sharp hate

you (still) send my way

and i get sick to my stomach because

your voice still haunts me telling me i still deserved it all

but they come less frequently now

and your ghost doesn't occupy the chair across from me

as much as it used to

nostalgia

this battlefield is empty now

no one occupies it but me

the ground is still bloodstained and

i still bear the marks of war

which are finally healing

scabbing over my mind

taking time to mend

and as i cross the terrain i stop for a second

to pick up a tattered

dirty paper and i open it

it's a letter i wrote to me

back when i was that thirteen-year-old girl

looking for some way to escape and she said

you can do it, just keep going

brin battisti

i feel so new

like a completely different person

now that everything i lay down on paper

no longer has a filter

-raw

nostalgia

i may not have

all the closure i desire but

i think we may finally be at peace with each other

i think you may be willing to stop trying to

get my attention

by saying and posting all this negativity

now that it's been made clear you can't hurt me anymore

and i have finally realized that

you can't hurt me anymore

and coming to this realization has given me all the power

i need

maybe one day

we can be friends again

this marks the beginning of not only a new year
but a brand-new decade

in the last ten years
i fought in a war i never thought
i'd have to fight
and as the smoke clears i finally can begin
to appreciate all the good that was happening
during that bad

i met some amazing people
lost others
i suffered what some threw at me
i endured
i accomplished things i'd never thought i would
and traveled to places i thought i'd never get to see
and here i am, lightweight and free and ready for what
the next decade has in store for me

-*january 1ˢᵗ, 2020*

nostalgia

the feeling of calm i have

for the first time in

a very long time

is almost overwhelming

i'm not used to the quiet serenity

but

on the days where

all i have is the chaos

at least i can

(almost) always

see the way out

at this time

seven years ago

that little girl i used to be was hopeless

with tired eyes and

a much too old for her age

four years ago

she was ready to stop caring

and ready to stop trying

she was ready to just go through the motions

with each day

and that was all

two years ago

there was some light

there was a faint glimmer of

the chance to live a life she

wanted

instead of being trapped in the tar pits

in the back of her mind

nostalgia

eight months ago

and that glimmer was gone and she thought

she was trapped forever with no way out

ever deserving of the

way she was being treated and that

she would never live up to

being enough

now

i have never been filled with more hope

those people along with their words

gone

and

who knows

sometime from now

maybe i'll finally be

completely

one hundred percent

free

now

i am nostalgic

i don't think of the horrors
the past had held
i just miss the feeling
of the untouched innocence
my childhood used to hold

nostalgia

you're stuck reliving the past too doll

it's not just me

i relive it through my poems

the ones that are

too much for you to handle

you relive it

by reading them

and trying to spark online fights

with the few people i have left that care about me

(after you made me push everyone else away)

you relive it by trying

to get a reaction from me

without realizing that is the *one thing*

i am smart enough not to give you

brin battisti

you weren't expecting

this

you weren't expecting me to

stand up, be strong, and walk away

you weren't expecting me to

see red

to get angry

to lash out

and be bold

-you were *expecting me to be* dead *though*

nostalgia

sometimes i still think of you

and all i remember was how sweet

you were on the outside

so sweet it was almost enough to

disguise the mess underneath

but blindly all i saw was the sugary sweet boy

you presented to me and

foolishly

i was stupid enough to take a bite and

all i got was a mouthful of rot

the sugar disintegrating as soon as it hit my lips

-some things take longer to forget

as well as i may be doing for myself now

please don't forget

i am also still fragile

at this moment in time

and as much as i talk about being a strong

fierce woman after coming out of it

it's a façade (for now)

it's motivation

to help push me forward

right now these scabs are still fresh

one thing

can push them open again and

i may crumble at the fingertips

of the one who does it

-handle with care

nostalgia

even ares would be proud

of the fight i just fought

-*god*dess *of war*

summer smiles at me and
she tells me in her warmth
that the ending of this chapter
will only begin
hundreds more

and within each
there will always be pain
pain isn't something you can hide from or avoid

but as long as i hold on and
i don't forget how far i came
i'll be able to conquer it all

nostalgia

i wept and mourned and grieved for you

and we were still in contact

i'm not sure exactly what we were doing

fumbling around the terms of our relationship

or

whatever we though we maybe had left

i had a pain in my chest and

it did not go away

until the fatal day it all blew up around us

like a nuclear bomb

the aftermath of our last exchange

left the space between us full of radiation and toxins

an unlivable atmosphere

and after that

i wept no more because you

wasted all my tears during the remaining time

we spent together, the seconds ticking down fast

-i knew trying to keep you was self-destruction

i am trying to move on

yes

and i desire to be let go entirely

but

there is just one thing i can't

seem to loosen my grip on

when will someone see me for who i am?

why is it that i am always stuck

with people telling me what i need to be

why can't i just show them who i am and

why isn't that good enough?

i am just so tired of being forced to shove down parts of
myself and

sacrifice everything i have for someone

who doesn't know anything about who i truly am and

forces me to be silent?

-this still hurts sometimes, despite it all

nostalgia

maybe me loving you

and

you maybe loving me

was our version of

mutually assured destruction

-mad

brin battisti

i felt this pain in my chest
similar to the feeling i had
when we were fumbling around each other for words
and walking on eggshells

when my friend showed me that picture of you today
it pains me to see you
(ironically) in the same state
you had put me in
(regardless of our past and what you've done to me)

and i feel like i should reach out
or check on you but
i know for the sake of my own mental health
i shouldn't
no
i can't
you'll have to find your own way this time

-moving forward

nostalgia

it may still hurt to think about you

and it will definitely still take me

sometime time to forgive, forget, and move on

and even more time to push down the desire

to reach out to you and offer

a friend to help you

but

i have no more tears

to cry when you cross my mind

and i think that

this is my body's way of starting the healing process

and my body's way of telling me

i will be okay

i don't need you to live

and i don't need to hold on to your words

-moving forward II

i talk a lot about wanting

one more final discussion with you

for closure or for a proper goodbye or something of that
sort but

if you were seated in front of me *(not allowed to talk,
just to listen)*

is it wrong of me to say

that i wouldn't *know*

what to say *(i'm not even sure where to begin)*

i would probably just

sit there and shake *(you still terrify me)*

and maybe i would just push all the boiling anger and

heated words back down into my belly

and ask if you were okay

ask how you were doing instead because

even now you still have

the ability to scare me into silence

nostalgia

i have had my heart

ripped to shreds by so many people

and i thought

maybe this time

with new friends and new people

it'll be better

but just like all the other times

i am not enough for them

i still don't fit in

i still get too upset and too sad and what can i do about it

i am beginning to think that maybe

i will just never

be enough

-lonely

*to the men who write about other women's pain and
glamourize it into something it's not:*

the only one who has the right

to write

about my pain is me

and the only one who has the right

to write

about her pain is her

and we won't romanticize the abuse the depression the
anxiety and the years of hardship we were put through
because

no one deserves to be put in that position and no one

should long to be like the girls that were in that position

my pain, her pain

is not something to just throw about and make other
young women wish they were like me, like her

-please leave her pain and mine, to us

nostalgia

when i first stepped out onto this battlefield

six years ago

i stepped out alone and

the only other person out here

was a reflection

of myself

the sky blood red and

everything else dull

dusty and colorless

almost like i was seeing in black and white

-the first battle

brin battisti

i hope and i pray
that those other people
the ones you claim are after me
aren't like you

aren't like the people in my poems
because those people
haven't done the same things to me
that all of you laying here in between my pages have

-there's a reason you're in my poems

(it's not a good one either)

nostalgia

that little thirteen-year-old girl
i hope that she's seeing how far i've come

and i hope she is proud of me

it's almost unusual

to not have this internal, eternal

turmoil

ping ponging across my thoughts anymore

there is a space

and it feels almost like i lost my only companion

the only way i know that

this is a good thing

is that i don't feel lonely or lost without it

i feel lighter

nostalgia

i'm finally coming out of the dark

and

i can finally see dawn

-it's beautiful

i keep going back and forth

and feeling so free yet

still drawn to the past in a way i

can't quite explain

but i know that eventually

i will no longer have to go back and forth

because i will be able to look my mistakes dead in the
face

and still be able to move on and accept where i have
been

and where i have come here

a message for all those other lost

hopeless thirteen-year-olds

who don't ever think they'll escape

you will

it will take time and effort and you may not see the light
out there just yet, but you will

even i still have my moments and still have bad days,
and i'm sure there are others out there even further along
on their journey than i am who still have their days too

the most important thing

is to just take your time don't rush, don't push, don't
force yourself to try and heal or forget or move on faster
than you should be. let things run its course

and you will see the dawn someday

the sun will shine her light on you again

and when you come out of that dark tunnel you will
glow, and you will be the most beautiful version of
yourself

the only one you need to impress love

is yourself

the summer breeze whispers in my ear
as she places a sunflower crown on my head

-light

nostalgia

with this sunflower crown i

declare this war over

declare myself queen and

i sit down at the round table with my

defeated enemies and

begin to work on our peace treaty

-light II

brin battisti

brin battisti

scars

&

peace treaties

nostalgia

time for my golden age of peace
and flourishing beauty

-and i lie my sword down

and as i take this scroll in my hands

dip the quill in the ink and

i begin to write

i write and i write and i write and

i don't stop until

i have finally finished making

the peace treaty i am

forcing myself to sign

so i never have to go to war again

and so i never live in darkness again

-*entente*

as the fall rolls around again

i breathe easy

i don't think i fear seeing you anymore

because i know

i am the one who

won

you forget that you

were the one who did

all you could and you did it

very publicly

and those caught in the middle and on the sidelines

who know all there is to know

still agreed that you were wrong, *not me*

and for those who don't know

i'll just you

marinate them with your lies

because i am done

entertaining you

-i'm not something for you to play with

i still have a lot of words that
i am not letting out on to these papers
for people to see
i realize that i must draw a line somewhere
as to what i let out
and what it may release if i do write those words down
and share them

i know some of my thoughts are too cruel and
too raging red hot
to even be honest and well thought out

i know
you will read this
and i know you will attack me for it
and i know you will be angry but at least i saved
the worst of it written down where
only i will ever be able to see the violent pain put into
those words

nostalgia

now

after years of being away from you

i know what your intentions with me were

you wanted me

to make her jealous and

it worked but

you will never know that

you're the one that broke me for the first time

used and sad and demolished

the words began to flow from the ashes

i can never understand why it had to be me

 but i suppose i should say thank you

for unleashing everything built up inside

now you get to see the queen you had a part in making

rise from the embers

now

after months if being away from you

i think i know what you trying to attain

you wanted me to be entirely under your control

and it didn't work so

you decided to take out the pent-up anger you had

out on me

you made it so that everything i did was a mistake

but you don't know that you let out the fire in my soul

i can never understand why it had to be me

that you needed to control, needed to manipulate

but i guess i should thank you too

for unleashing the voice i didn't know i needed

now you too, get to see the queen you had a part in
making

put your embers out

nostalgia

i write about you

and then i rewrite those poems again and again

and although you may have a resting place

among my pages

you no longer have a home in my head

or in my heart

and that's the most important thing

it is never too late

to let the voice deep down inside you

finally come out

nostalgia

i will never again

be ashamed of the scars and the damage

those years of battle

gave me

those wounds healed over time

and that damage

began to be fixed over time

they taught me that nothing is

un-survivable if you fight hard enough

never allow any person to tell you what you are worth

because only you

should ever be in charge of how you see your beauty,
courage, kindness, creativity, intelligence, and self.

-agreement I

i spend a lot of time

trying to *(instead of torture myself)*

reflect

on the past

somedays, it doesn't go very well *(i end up torturing)*

but most days, i am finally able to learn

i reflect, i gather, and then

i let go

brin battisti

now is as good a time as any
to finally work on becoming
the strong
independent
outspoken woman
i need to be

nostalgia

depression

i was depressed

and i was stuck inside for a long time

i know the cause, it was because i knew i lost myself

and acknowledging that fact made it that much more real, that much harder to dig myself out of the pit i fell into headfirst

but going through heartbreak one, two, three, four times, made it worse than i ever thought it would be and

none of them could ever even understand because i couldn't be bothered to explain to them how they were hurting me or how they did hurt me

i just crawled into a shell and i hid like a coward because

i had given up, it seemed like no matter what i would always lose the people i loved and scare away the friends i thought i needed to save me and so

there i was, helpless and numb and too afraid to fix it

-five stages of grief IV

when i finally got off the battlefield the first thing i did

was destroy all my weapons

i decided that today was the day

i would stop attacking myself

for things far out of my control

nostalgia

learn to accept the fact that you will never be able to control the thoughts, actions, and motives of another person

if they truly love you, you won't feel as though you must go to war with yourself and

if they truly love you, they won't hurt you in all the ways you were hurt before

but you cannot control their love

so if they show you they don't love you

leave.

-agreement II

brin battisti

i think i knew in the back of my mind

we were going to be a train wreck

when i told you

you make me hate myself

and you didn't understand

-hindsight

nostalgia

i said that a part of me
still loves you
and i would like to correct that

a part of me loves you
for the never-ending flow of words
your damage provided me

a part of me loves you
for the feeling of freedom and
the sweet taste of power my senses were
flooded with
when you released me

and a part of me loves you
for all of the lessons i learned and
for showing me how i should never allow
another soul to treat me again

brin battisti

fall usually means
the end of life
things are dying and
preparing for the cold harsh winter but

this time to me
all i can see this fall
is the excitement and joy

for what next spring will bring for me
and closing peace
now knowing that the end of the year this time
won't be a brutal beating

it will be sweet and soft nostalgia
and nothing more

-full circle

nostalgia

i know that i am making progress

because

whenever you come up in conversation nowadays

my heart doesn't kick start and

i don't shrink away or hide

from fear that your name means that

you're near somewhere

i always wondered if i

would ever find someone that would love

every single part of myself

i didn't realize that person

was supposed to be me

all along

nostalgia

i used to spend

long endless nights

thinking that in alternate lives

alternate universes

maybe we worked

and maybe *we are*

not *we were*

and in those other worlds it was all perfect

in those worlds i didn't lose anyone

i would still have all of my

friends and family and loved ones

by my side

but

if in an alternate universe

i still had all these ghosts with me for real

i know i wouldn't be here

i wouldn't be better

actually

i would be much worse

if i were surrounded by all

the people that

made me feel worthless

i know i'd have dug myself

into a hole so deep no one

would be able to pull me out

not even myself

-this is why alternate universes don't exist

nostalgia

be grateful and remember

the things you do have

and stop mourning the loss of the things you used to
have

sometimes it takes losing those aspects of your life

to clear a much better path

for you to walk on

not all loss is tragic

-agreement III

the process of healing isn't something that you just wish
would happen, and it does, it doesn't happen overnight,
immediately, and you can't expect to see results in 24
hours, like some miracle medicine. the process of
moving on is the same way. the past will always have a
way of tricking your mind into holding on and thinking,
and in order to go on, sometimes you must listen, but not
dive too deep.

nostalgia

i finally hear

what my poems

have been trying to tell me

today is the day the queen

with the sunflower crown

puts herself first

she can't grow

without giving herself the same love and support

that she gives to her flowers

if anyone ever tries to tie their sick little puppet strings around you ever again, you take a match and you burn those strings. you take a match and you burn them to the ground. you are not some object, and you are not a pawn in their game of chess.

queens are not controlled.

-agreement IV

i never expected a peace treaty

to be so hard to write

considering the only person that must sign

is myself

but i suppose after the war i just had

this is something that is

much needed

nostalgia

there are some occasions where

the ghosts on your battlefield are better off just that,

ghosts.

but sometimes

the best thing you can do is reach out to someone

(as long as they didn't try to sink you to the bottom of an ocean)

and bring their ghost back to life

-i'm glad you came back

brin battisti

as each sun rises

realize that there are good days and bad days

just as there are rainy days and sunny days

learn to live in the present and

cherish what you have because

before you know it

those moments will be gone

forgotten with time

and you will regret letting the good times

slip out of your grasp

it's okay to take a step back and breathe. in order to grow, you need to allow yourself some moments of solitude, moments of peace, moments of reflection. but it is also important to know that in those moments of reflection, you can't linger, you can't overthink. reflection doesn't mean self-torture. learn from the mistakes, then move on and better yourself from them.

if you don't let go, you'll drown again.

-agreement V

brin battisti

we all have the strength

and the souls

of the bravest warriors out there

we will endure and we will survive

no matter who tries to kill us

nostalgia

i remember once i read a poem where

the poet compared her scars

to tiger stripes

and i remember thinking

how can she possibly think that

they aren't pretty and

they aren't something i feel proud of

years later i think i understand

it's not that they are pretty

it's that they're symbols of strength

each one a different battle and the fact that i can tell the story

means that i won in the end

it's not that you're proud of what you did

but you're proud you made it through

they aren't something you flaunt

but they are reminders of what you've dealt with

brin battisti

for her, her scars were tiger stripes because
she is a tiger
an animal fierce and bold
and *strong*

for me i now think of them as battle scars
for the war, my mind was playing out in my head
for the struggles and fears and damage and pain
i went through on my own

in the end
it was me coming out on top and
my story is proof that
you can make it through the war zone

if there are red flags, warning signs, and things that suggest that a person is not as they seem, stop being naïve. stop ignoring them. stop thinking it will be better tomorrow, and after months and months it's still not. at that point it's no longer optimism, it's stupidity. if a person says they'll change, let them change on their own time, and make them prove it to you, instead of letting them walk all over you until you're beaten to the ground and broken all over again.

you are better than that, you don't deserve that trauma.

not again.

-agreement VI

this right here
and everything you are holding in your hands
is the most honest i have ever been with myself
about the condition i was in
about my feelings and emotions and problems
and for a lot of it
these pages are the first time i am allowing myself to
stop denying and ignoring
how bad i really was

this is my story, and this is it
unfiltered and honest and raw
and this is me
telling myself the truth for the first time
and i didn't expect admitting it all
to feel so freeing

nostalgia

lay me down in a bed of ash
and rather than crumble with the dust

i will build a city

knowing that

i fought the pain and

i came out on top

is all the closure

this queen needs

-i don't need to hear it from anyone but myself

nostalgia

it's been roughly five years that i spent

tripping in and out of traps laid out for me

and climbing halfway up a mountain only to fall back down to the bottom again

5 years is

60 months

approximately 261

1,827 days

43,848 hours

2,630,880 minutes and

157,852,800 seconds

of war

and

only

three months

free

(best three months of my life)

brin battisti

when i first stepped out onto this battlefield

five years ago

there was no one but me

the sky bloodred

everything else dusty and dull

colorless

and i was moving

in slow motion

just trying to face each new hour as it came

not really noticing the turn of each day

twilight and dawn

had no difference

-day one

nostalgia

i close the door

lock it tight and

then

i break the doorknob anyway (just in case)

then i go get those iron bars and

i weld them

across the doorframe too (precautionary measures)

lock in all that trauma behind that door to

keep myself from perusing the selection

and getting sucked into the reaching grasp

of despair again

ironically, symbolically

i wear the key of the broken doorknob around my neck

i like to think of it as me taunting those reaching vines

the same way they would dangle the sunlight or those

scissors

brin battisti

just out of my grasp, when i couldn't escape

now though

the vines have nowhere to go

and i can hold the key

just in front of the door and show them

how they'll never get out of that door

while i hold the scissors

i (finally) had stolen back in one hand

and

the

sunlight

in

the

other

nostalgia

now as i step out onto this same field

five years later

i realize the dusty colorless place i once knew

is covered in

vibrant bright yellow sunflowers

and when i look back up

i'm surrounded by people

who love me for who i am inside

and only when i loved myself was i able

to see and appreciate the love they had for me

and now there's not a ghost in sight

-day one thousand nine hundred

at nineteen years old

i can finally say that i am

so

      very

           proud

               of

                    all

              i

      managed

to

survive

through

i feel beautiful

and i feel radiant

i feel like if you were to turn the lights off

or dump me in the middle of the darkest abyss

i'd still shine so bright

i've *never*

felt so *healthy* before

not just physically

(i no longer get that sick feeling in the pit of my stomach)

but *emotionally*

i just feel like i can fly

and i feel such an astronomical amount of *strength*

emanating from my core to the rest of my body

i finally feel in control, in charge

and tears of pure joy spill from my eyes

as i take of my shoes

and i let down my hair

and i dump all of the masks of

fake happiness because

i no longer need them

and i just run and *run*

because i can, because i'm no longer tied down

barefoot across this gorgeous field of sunflowers and
grass

and i feel my soul soar high above the clouds

this feeling of elation almost (almost)

overwhelming

the years of harsh words and cold evaporated from my
mind

and i *finally*

just feel beautiful

nostalgia

dear future,

whatever you may hold for me
i am ready to take it on
now that the fear in my heart
is gone

dear future,

beware
because this girl boiling with revenge
is coming for you

brin battisti

nostalgia

brin battisti

sunflower girl

nostalgia

i feel like a girl made of magic

a girl with eyes shimmering with stardust

a girl as radiant as a sunflower

a girl in control

-birth of a sunflower girl

brin battisti

and through the sunflowers
i was born again

nostalgia

i take my past

and i stuff it into trash bags

bring it to the curb and i don't think twice

when i let them take it away

this was never nostalgia

it was torture

and i no longer want myself to

take part

once upon a time there was a girl

who didn't believe she had what it took

to be loved by anyone

and

if no one else loved her

why would she love herself

that is when lady earth

took her soul and

she planted her among the sunflowers

and told her she will always shine bright

as long as she stayed true to herself

acceptance:

i have finally come to peace and i have finally stopped holding on

all those people i lost

they came and went from my life and

they served their purpose for me

they taught me their lessons and they were there when i needed them, at just the right moment

now it is time for the last grasps of their memories

to turn to dust at the touch of my fingertips and

it is time for other people to find them

right now it's time to focus on me

it's time to become the best possible version of myself

and i can't do that if i am holding on to you all

for even a moment longer

i've accepted that you are all gone and i am ready to move on

-final stage of grief

brin battisti

the moment i finally flew free

my body was overwhelmed

with the immense amount of joy

i felt after all these years

nostalgia

i didn't just wake up one morning

perfectly okay and

all signs of what i'd been through

were magically erased from my mind

but i did wake up one morning and realize that

the first thing on my mind wasn't

sadness or fear or helplessness

the first thing on my mind was the feeling

of being content in my own skin and

happy with the place i'm in

the process was slow

it wasn't easy

and i can't say the past doesn't still live in the back
corners of my mind

but as time went on i began to take note of the little
things

one day i smiled a bit more than usual

or yesterday i laughed harder than i had in a while

or even that i was more open to someone

and as this all began adding up

i started treasuring those moments

looking eagerly for the next time i can feel that elation

and realizing the ghosts stopped peeking around corners

and the ropes they tied around me were gone

and eventually i realized

i wasn't sad anymore

and if something did upset me

it didn't stay with me nearly as long as it would have

even six months ago

nobody but me

knows my whole story

but i think i can finally say the past is in the past

i came out alive

and i look forward

to each new dawn

nostalgia

on each scar

a sunflower blossomed

to remind me that

no matter what had happened

i'm here now

and nothing else matters

the past can't be changed
and I understand that now

so i just pick the dead flowers out of my hair
and wait for the new ones to grow

nostalgia

i didn't love myself yet

and so i put that responsibility on to others

and they all just showed me that

that wasn't fair of me to do that to them

but they also showed me why

i *shouldn't* do that

they all just crushed my spirit

so i learned how to love myself after all

brin battisti

talking to the sunflowers

ı think that thirteen-year-old girl

with the lonely heart

and the sad eyes discovered

that her journey was meant to be hers

it was made for her

and she doesn't know why exactly she was put

through the war of a lifetime

but she knows now

she was made to come out on top

and when her sadness died on the battlefield

the acres of those sunflowers came to life

showing her at the end of the darkness

comes a world of light

nostalgia

i am beginning to believe

i didn't find poetry

it found me

because this is the only way
i've been able to cope

the poet entered my soul at the very moment i needed
her

and she seared her mark into my heart

and she made her exit

leaving the words flowing from my fingertips

brin battisti

i don't wear makeup to hide anymore

i don't need it to cover my

dark circles and

sickly colored skin

stained grey from the sleepless nights

instead i wear

barely any at all

i let it accentuate the newfound happiness in my eyes

the brightness in my smile

and i let my natural glow

shine through

nostalgia

sunlight will always come again child

just look to the north and

over the horizon

and the world will be light again

the sun's flowers whispered to me

-sunflower child

brin battisti

i like being the one in charge

of my self-love

self-image

and my destiny

nostalgia

i met a sunflower boy

who taught me that i didn't need to be loved intimately

to be loved wholly

who taught me that beauty is most important

on the inside

who taught me that it's okay to be unsure and

to take my time

-sunflower boy

brin battisti

i don't look at my battle scars and feel disgusted
anymore

i look at them and

i feel a sweetness

i feel like sugar and warmth all sticky and good

because i know what i've overcome

in spite of all of you

who threw me to the ground and ripped me to shreds

nostalgia

you love me so freely

my soul has never flown higher

i cannot express enough how glad i am

you aren't like the others

to chase me with rope and torches and chains

to keep me in your clutches

you let me live

and i have never been happier

-thank you for understanding

brin battisti

with you

i feel all the fear

leave my lungs

and all the terror

drain from my heart

leaving me feeling

like warm molasses inside

my sunflower boy

you showed me that love isn't

living scared

shaking and on the verge of tears every time you come near

it's not meant to be prison

it's meant to take flight

you simply took my hands and you told me

you will show me all the good in the world

and you will help me

learn exactly how much

i am actually worth

to the people who love me the most

-sunflower boy II

brin battisti

never again will i ever

sugar coat nostalgia

-i learned that the hard way

nostalgia

love will show itself in millions of forms throughout the
lifetimes we will walk

sometimes the love of another person will help us learn
undiscovered parts of ourselves

other times the love you feel for someone will be used
against you

but it's only meant to make you grow

and sometimes

it's the love you need to give yourself

when you really need it most

i think i'm beginning to understand

why everyone talks about their pain

triumphantly

because i am so damn proud

of what i managed to fight through

nostalgia

this is the first time
i am ever openly admitting to
what i went through
nobody ever knew the full extent

until now

and to some it may not be a big deal
another cliché poem about surviving an epic battle
something not nearly as bad as what others went through

but for me
it was a huge step to choose to let it spill across these
pages
my heart is laid out here

-handle with caution

brin battisti

i am slowly learning
my self-worth

and in this process i'm learning
no one else *deserves* a say
in who i am

nostalgia

like flowers in the middle of the desert

too much time

spent out in the heat

will kill you

*-stop interrogating your past, you have nothing to gain
from it*

brin battisti

it is time

to let go of all the

fear

plaguing your mind

and step out into the sunlight

where your truest beauty will show

nostalgia

we lay together

my head on your lap and

your fingers tangled in my hair

and i have never felt

such a sweet silence before

-you show me love in all the right ways

i was a wreck

and i still kind of am

after him

but you show me such kindness and patience, i can't
remember the last time someone has been so gentle with
me. you let me grow on my own, you let me have my
time.

you listen to my endless worries and fears and sit
through my millions of apologies and the frequent
interruptions so i can ask if you are okay, and to make
sure i didn't do anything wrong. it's all just become a
habit, a result of the damage.

you quietly tell me that we are going to fix what has
been broken, and i am going to do it on my own, with
your support by my side.

i cannot thank you enough for all you have given, after
so much has been taken

-*how can i possibly repay you*

nostalgia

seeing all these

unfiltered parts of me

scares me

i know some people will be angry

and others confused

and others who hate

all that i have said

but

this was something i needed to do

because the unfiltered truth

is the unfiltered me

and i want to become the

most real and honest version of myself

-it all starts here

brin battisti

what is it with you and sunflowers

someone asked me the other day

*they remind me of happiness and strength and to stand
tall and proud*

i tell them

they fill me with hope for a better tomorrow

and the sunflowers offer me protection

from all the harsh uncertainties that are bound to come

-sunflower girl

nostalgia

the confidence i feel

flowing through my body

is so addicting

and i wonder

what made feeling this way so hard?

i think we're all

looking for a little bit of hope

especially now

when the world just feels like it's going to

i m p l o d e

at any moment

my hope stems from the rush of

the sweetness i get

biting into freedom

the taste spilling over my lips

the heat spreading from my belly throughout my whole
body

nostalgia

real love

is the kind that loves

without hurting

without destroying

without killing

the other

the sweet summer air runs her cool fingers

across my cheeks

and the sunflowers dance before me

the dandelions are plump with new wishes

eagerly waiting to be made and

my soul is alive with new belief

the magic i used to long die

has come back to me

and all i had to do was

believe in myself first

nostalgia

to all the people

who are for some reason

pitted against me, dead set on watching me fall

in case you missed it, i already fell and now

i am rising above you and

i am already so much farther ahead in life

than you could even imagine

and if you even thought for one second

that i am not used to being the odd one out

and i am not used to everything being stacked against me

you're wrong

but you are all no longer even the slightest bit relevant to
me

so keep talking

it'll only help me build myself higher anyway

i have already accomplished more

than i had ever

thought i could

i will no longer allow

anyone

to take that away from me

-pride

nostalgia

it is time for me

to stop running back into the

dark and angry and sad

embrace of yesterday

and start running

towards the

sugar sweet, warm, promising, sunflower yellow

embrace of tomorrow

-renewed spirit

brin battisti

it never took much
to push me off the cliff

and it took a hell of a fight
to climb back up again

and now that i am here
i have iron clad boots
wrapped in the roots of the wildflowers and trees
securing me to the ground

to make sure
        i never
ever
        fall like that
ever again

nostalgia

you were the first person

to let me heal me

without placing this heroic stigma upon me

without seeing me as your damsel in distress

and without feeling you were the one who needed to be
my savior

you were the first one to understand

that only i

could mend what was broken inside me

and you are willing to let me do that

and i can't thank you enough

for showing love to even the broken parts inside me

-sunflower boy III

with him,

I felt fear

and i labeled it as love

with you

there just is no fear

only love

-sunflower boy IV

nostalgia

i think i knew

that we were going to be different

that day you came in and found me
on the floor and crying
my heart racing and my breathing so ragged from all the
pain and fear i was feeling

when you pulled me into your arms and didn't say
i'll fix it, i will make it better

but you said instead
you'll be okay and you'll get through this
and that
i'll always be here for you when you need me

-you gave me the freedom to write my own story

brin battisti

the sunflowers gave me my crown

and you gave me my laughter back

and myself?

i gave myself a new beginning

-the sunflowers and you

happiness should never come

at the highest cost you can afford to pay

you should never sacrifice the stability of your mental
health

your self-worth

and who you are because the truth is

true happiness doesn't come with those prices

brin battisti

dear sunflower boy,

thank you for teaching me that
i can love other people
and love myself
the right way
at the same time

nostalgia

i don't live in black and white

in captivity

chained to a basement

in the dark

or alone anymore

and that's how i know

the worst of it is over

and i the warrior, has emerged to the other side

victorious

brin battisti

update:

i kind of like looking at myself in the mirror today
dressed in the yellow dress
with my hair braided with wildflowers
topped off with my sunflower crown

looking like joy

not only do i know who i really am

i know the power i hold

in the center of my palm and

laced around my fingertips

it's the pieces

of the goddesses i wished and prayed i could be

all the princesses i longed to become

all the fairies and whimsical creatures

all of the models and celebrities i desired to stand with

i have my own magic and i have my own voice

i have the beauty of all the wishes cast when i was
younger deep down inside me

and like a sunray bursting through the clouds

i'm ready to unleash it all into this world

-goddess within

i am tired of writing
to the sensitivities of other people

i let them quiet and hush what i had to say
in order to preserve relationships and save people
from the truth i needed to speak

and i am no longer going to allow
anyone to quiet my voice anymore
because here it is
all the years of built up and pushed down truth and
all of what needed to be said
spilled across these pages all at once

you cannot quiet the voices inside
and so i finally stopped trying to do just that

nostalgia

time for me

to let the wolf and fire

buried down deep inside

out into this fragile world

and it's time for people

to start listening to the truth

instead of hiding behind pretty metaphors

and glorified trauma

the only person i really want to get to know right now

is the woman living inside me

who finally can grow and stand tall

flower and bloom through disarray

i want to take her out to coffee

ask her how her day is

and how discovering who she is

is going

i want to get to know her new standards and morals

have a conversation about pain

know what she loves and

what she hates

i want to go for a walk with her and

i want to learn all about who she is going to be

because this is the part

where i finally transform

-sunflower queen

nostalgia

with her i want to grow

i want to listen to music with her

get to know why she loves the messages behind the
words

and watch movies and take her out to dinner

i want to show her that i really can love myself

without anyone else's verification

a nod yes in approval to tell me i'm worthy

i want to be the one who lets them

plead and fight to show me

that they are worthy enough for me and the women i
want to become

to share our love with them

and i want to get to watch the sunflowers bloom in the
springtime

into the magical crown she'll place on her head once she
and i

become one

-*sunflower queen II*

brin battisti

brin battisti

letters to the past

nostalgia

brin battisti

i have decided

being nostalgic and

constantly reliving the past

isn't my thing

nostalgia

i must admit

i am quite terrified to write these letters

they are far too specific

far too filled with pain

for these ghosts to not know that

these poems are about them

if they ever decide

to get their hands on this

but i have to write it out

so i can let these final burdens go

i will never get another conversation

nor do i want one with some of these people

so this is the moment

i will say what is on my mind and

i will release all the final unsaid things

into the night

                              if you choose to read them

tread carefully please

and do not seek me out afterwards

because this is it

this is that final step i need to take

after this

after this chapter has been written

i am closing the book

sealing it tight

and i am going to go live

in the now

like i should have been doing

all along

nostalgia

i sit down in a circle

surrounded by all of the ghosts

of people i once knew, people i once loved

and with a quiet voice

shaking and nervous i begin to speak to them

the time has come for me to let you all go. i have to move on and the only way i can do that is to lock the doors and windows to the entryways of my mind, i must have a 'no ghosts allowed' policy and i must follow it. the sake of my mental health depends on it.

i have one final message for each of you, call it what you will, but it isn't closure, because i suppose, to get that, i'll need to hear your final messages as well, and none of you are really here, it's all an illusion anyway. the moment my fingertips leave these letters, is the moment your access to haunt me is taken away.

for my own sake

i need you all to vanish

and then i pick up my basket of letters, and i begin to call out their names

none of these letters were easy to write

but they were all bottled up inside

so please be delicate

this is the most vulnerable

i have ever chosen to be

nostalgia

you were probably my favorite ghost

because we were such great friends

before

-how do i tell you that when we haven't spoken in so
long?

ghost #1

you don't know about anything i have gone through,
since we spoke last. your final conversation was when
we were sixteen, three years ago, and we were both lost.
and so in order to let you go, i have to say i am so sorry.
i am sorry for losing you as my best friend, and as one of
the most important people in my life.

i still miss you, and i still think about you often

but it isn't healthy for me to keep wondering how you
are

when you just decided to leave without warning

nostalgia

i will do

whatever i must

to keep myself from falling back into that black and
white abyss

you may come to me

wanting reconciliation

hoping to maybe rekindle the dead embers of

whatever friendship or relationship we had in the past

but the most i will give you is forgiveness

and after that

not a second glance

the only way to clean my system of poison

is to stop feeding into it in the first place

brin battisti

maybe you need to let me go
just as much as i need to let you go

and maybe it's time
i faced that

nostalgia

you still haunt me

to this day you scare me

you took things that weren't meant for you to take

you showed me what real love felt like

and you showed me what real pain was too

i can't ever, *ever* forgive you for what you did to me

and i can't even say that it still doesn't hurt

three years later

because it still burns

but i have to forget you

so *i* stop picking at the mangled scar tissue

i still have as a result of *you*

ghost #2

our story was short lived. and immediately i regretted falling so fast. i maybe should have seen it coming, that all the lies you were feeding me were too good to be true. i didn't expect heartbreak to hurt so bad, but because of you i cried so hard i was sick, i couldn't eat for weeks, and i cried for months.

i remember each and everything you said to me. one night you asked me if i could do anything in that moment of time, what would i do. i had said i don't know. you, on the other hand, said you would marry me. two weeks later, you forced yourself onto me. a week after that, you were gone.

you took so much from me and even worse, the lies that you told anyone you talked to, after. not only did you destroy me and shatter me and take something that wasn't even meant to be yours, you bragged about it. you hurt me in a way i never wanted to hurt again

i want you to know, i don't forgive you. i may never forgive you. but i won't allow you to live on in my writing or in my life any longer. the best thing for you is to erase you from everything.

i hope you know what you did, and i hope it destroys you inside. then, i hope you learn, and i hope you treat whoever comes next a million times better. from now on, i am done with everything having to do with you.

nostalgia

i no longer have these

wispy tendrils of the past with me

they are stored in a trash bag

in the corner of my mind

a foggy memory

i need to remember

that though they are gone

i am still here

and my purpose in life

was not to live for them

it is to live for me

-still thriving

they used to suck the very life out of my bones
leaving me hollow and dull inside
collapsing to the floor in an exhausted
worn out heap of
girl and tears

and when they left
i still blamed myself

but now i feel like i could fly to the sun
and run across the world

and they aren't here to take that away anymore

-i know it wasn't me now

nostalgia

i really truly miss you all

but what is there left for me to possibly do?

ghosts #6-? (to all the friends that drifted away)

there was a reason you were all in my life, and maybe you were only meant to stay, for a short amount of time. regardless, the time has since long past, for me to stop clinging on to all of you. i have to stop missing you and wishing you were here with me because you aren't anymore.

i am finally ready to accept that you all moved on with your lives, and now it's time for me to move on with mine, too.

nostalgia

if the world were to end in a week

and i had the chance to mend everything with everyone

you are the one ghost

i wouldn't bother reviving

you killed me dead months ago

and in return

i killed you dead in my poems

trying to eradicate the most abusive months of my life

through my writing

ghost #3

you are the last person i want to write to. but i have so much left unsaid, so much anger, so much pain built up inside still, after our fiery explosion of an ending.

you had no right to treat me the way you did. no right to manipulate, fold, and form me into the person you thought i should be. a quiet and compliant little girl who would do what she was told. maybe that was the reason this didn't work out. because i wanted at least some leeway, and you offered none, slapping tighter and tighter restraints across my wrists, every time i fought.

to whoever comes next for you, i already know what you will tell them. that i was the one who destroyed your trust, i was the abusive one, i was despicable, i was horrendous, and i didn't love you.

but the proof of my love should have been the fact that i stayed after every loaded question, every interrogation, every finger pointed at me, every backhanded apology, every time you told me i was never allowed to do something. those who matter most know where the responsibility lies. you took everything. the sliver of self-love i was beginning to develop. my stability around anyone else. my happiness. you took and took and took and in return justified it with material objects.

now i am taking it all back, without you.

ghost #3

i still have nightmares about you, that's one part that won't leave me alone

i can move on, i can leave you behind, i can do it all, but i can't help that the moment someone mentions your name

you appear in my dreams ready to *kill*

ghost #3

i try not to hate people, but i hate *you*

for all that you put me through

i can never and will never write enough letters because there are so many things left i want to say, and yet i know, no matter how many letters i write, no matter how many speeches i have prepared, you will never truly listen to what i am trying to say. i desperately want to say it all anyway

in order to make up for the year i let you silence me completely. in order to make up for the hundreds of times i just gave up instead of standing up for myself in order to make up for not fighting. not walking away. for staying so much longer than i should have. maybe to try and get closure with my own mind, for putting my soul through all of it much longer than i should have. for not taking care of myself like i should have.

i am not really sure why i feel the need to get it all out there, but i do, and so here it all is.

-i'll try to leave it at that

p.s.

you are not, and will not, be forgiven.

only forgotten.

that is all i have left to give out to you

i love recklessly

and i don't take caution

when i should

and then in the end

the person i assigned the name *love* to

leaves again

their ghost remaining to haunt my dreams

but i am tired of giving my love to people

that cannot handle the full force

of all that i am

love isn't a name

love isn't a specific someone

so i must stop labeling love to your name

nostalgia

i think the reason

i had always felt so lonely

was because i have always surrounded myself

with people who don't exist anymore

as a way to hold on

they'd work themselves into my dreams and

i don't have to feel lonely anymore

because i'm surrounded by

real people

who really love me this time

brin battisti

i wasn't entirely ready to write this letter to you yet
because i still missed you
just a little

nostalgia

this one was my fault

and for that

i am so sorry

ghost #4

you came into my life not once, or twice, but three different times. the first time, i never really got to know you as well as i should have. the second time, you were a person i needed at just the right moment and the third time, i loved you.

i shouldn't have pushed you away, the way i did. i pushed you so far, you ended up leaving, when really all i needed was your comfort.

i was selfish and i didn't even begin to consider what you may have been going through or that maybe you needed support from someone too. i shouldn't have been as surprised as i was when it all ended, and you cut me out for good. all i want you to know is that, i would never lie to you, and i never meant to hurt you.

i just need you to know that this guilt has been weighing on my chest for two years, and even if you never see this letter, i am so sorry for closing you out. for being selfish, and for putting you through the exact same pain i was going through myself.

i hope with all my heart that one day you can forgive me.

nostalgia

these ghosts,

having those

c a r e f u l l y

p a i n s t a k i n g l y

written letters

held in their misty hands

begin to

f a d e a w a y

slowly evaporating from the circle

and a cool breeze runs through my hair

and i feel safer

the room a bit warmer

i stand here, basket in hand, relieved

that most of what i had to say

has been said

i take a trip to my flourishing garden
and with the fresh roses in my hands i lay them down
one by one
side by side
and the last breath of each and every
long gone soul
living within me
exists my body

today is my last day of mourning
and tomorrow
is the first day
of my very own
brand new story

-regrowth

nostalgia

i've never taken advantage of each new sunrise before

i'd used to long for the sunrises of yesterday

and of months ago

thinking that with each day

if i could just go back

i could change and fix everything

i wouldn't have gone through all that pain

if i could just change who i had been

around all the people i've lost

then i would be perfect

and no one will think that i'm not worth it

i need to give up trying to be what everyone else wants
me to be

because it's not who i was *meant* to become

and so with the ghosts

i let the voices go too

brin battisti

you're the one

that i have the most to lose with

because you are brand new

you emerged the moment i broke my chains

and set myself free

nostalgia

to the ghost of the girl i used to be

i had everything taken from me. i had my happiness, i had my trust, my belief in magic and good. i had what i thought love was supposed to be, destroyed. i missed being a little girl without a fear and a care in the world. i missed having my innocence.

i retreated in fear of change. i cowered in a dark corner of my mind, trying to salvage the last remaining scraps of childish notion. i clung to these scraps with tears running down my face and sadness oozing from my pores for years. i spoke and dreamt of the ghosts of those i lost. i whispered that in another world, i had magic, i had talent, i had true love, i had it all.

and now that i have begun to come to terms with the way real life actually works, i know i have to let go. i have to unclench my fists, let those scraps fly away, taken somewhere with the wind. i need to accept that i am not a secret mermaid in disguise, i am not a powerful Disney princess that has ice powers, i am not someone that has the kind of magic i used to dream about and long for.

however, i have my own kind of magic deep down inside me, and that magic is what got me here. i may not be innocent, but i have to thank my lucky starts that, by being exposed to all this pain and all the darkness surrounding this world, i am also not ignorant.

eventually, we all come face-to-face with real life. we all shed the skin of being children and we are all faced with adulthood. my magic, is still being able to trust, still seeing the good, and still see light and stardust and being able to realize there is still hope out there somewhere.

i have to stop fearing change because that is all we can rely on. with every change comes the opportunity for better. and for me, with every change came a step towards a deeper happiness that i can grasp.

i no longer want to live with the reminder of what i allowed people to reduce me to. i don't want to constantly fear that i will become that sad, lonely, broken girl again. i have to thank her for all of the lessons she taught me, and then i have to let her go along with all of the daydreams and desperate attempts to hold on to what has changed long ago.

i am on a much better path now, and with each step i take forward, the brighter my future looks.

nostalgia

i place my pen down

i seal off the final letter

and i distribute the rest of them out to each ghost

and with each letter that leaves my possession

my heart feels

l

i

g

h

t

e

r

my mind

u n c l o u d   i n g

this hazardous fog

c l e a r i n g

and i know that i made it to the next sunrise

i go into my tiny home

and i break out the cleaning supplies

and i begin to scrub as hard as i can

spring cleaning

i whisper to myself

washing washing washing away

the dusty cobwebs

that formed in the corners i used to avoid because

the ghosts were there

i redecorate with flowers

hang up my fairy lights

take down horrid pictures

and i open the curtains

allowing the sun to wash over the parts i'd kept in the dark

-spring cleaning

after i finish my cleaning

i decided to clean myself too,

just for good measure

i step into the piping hot shower and i scrub and scrub
and scrub my skin

two, three, four times

to wash away years of different touches and sadness

that etched its way deep into my body

some things

i can't wash away

but i've grown to love them as the part of myself

that fought and that won

so i don't mind those parts so much anymore

and once i step out of the water, my skin raw and red

i was never as refreshed and free as i am now

-spring cleaning II

brin battisti

a letter to those still healing

remember to keep breathing

and appreciate the process

you can't mend those wounds overnight

these things take time

so just breathe and keep your head up

and you will get there

nostalgia

i must admit

i myself am also to blame

for all the pain

i hurt myself

when i would look in the mirror and criticize every flaw,
despising everything i was, envious of all i did not have

i cannot go on if i cannot accept

that who i am and the qualities i possess are ones that
were given to me

i have to carry myself proudly

because i am the only one that

i should rely on for making my own joy and happiness

and i will not get very far

if i don't love who i am

-epiphany

brin battisti

to the ghosts that will come later

i am no longer wasting my heart
on those who will abuse it
i have some walls put up
boundaries set in place
warning signs all around

and i won't waste my heart on mourning you
once you've left
the paranormal investigators are in
and i will ensure that every last ghost
has left for good

i no longer have the energy to weep for those that don't
want or love every part of me

nostalgia

i never want to question who i am

or feel the way i did

when i was with you

i was terrified, sad, and i loathed the creature

you convinced me i was

i had never hated myself more

and i should have recognized sooner

what you were doing to me

but i have taken notes

i faced myself in the mirror

i cradled my bleeding heart and i told her

if i am any kind of creature

i will embody the goddess of war

the goddess of beauty

-i have never been more powerful

i will show the world i was never as disgusting

and you told them i am

i am lit on fire

and full of spite and courage and revenge

and i am not weak anymore

i am not silent, i am not ugly

and it took all you hurled at me

to get here

so i must ask

do you like the result of what you created?

are you happy, proud even?

that instead of crumbling, i rose from every single
beatdown ever inflicted on me

with a raging power inside

-i have never been more powerful II

nobody can tell my story

the same way i can

so i want to make sure this story ends

with the once broken girl

knowing how to love herself the way

no one else can

with that once scared little girl

fearless and bold and strong

with that once desperate little girl craving for someone to
come save her

carried off into the sunset by nothing else

but her own two feet

with the once sad little girl

as exuberant and radiant as ever

her own lover, savior, queen, and friend

through all these years

i learned that i should never underestimate anyone's
ability to change

the saying that people never change is a lie

everyone has to change in order to adapt

i have changed in order to end up where i am today, and
everyone i have ever known has also changed, whether it
be for better or for worse

i don't fear change anymore

i am eager for change to embrace me in her arms

take my hand

and show me the way

i feel like a princess

at the end of a fairytale

i finally have everything i ever wanted

and i have come

so far

-happy endings

brin battisti

this is where
my life finally begins
for real this time

-stepping forward

nostalgia

i take a trip to my flourishing garden

and with the fresh roses in my hands i lay them down

one by one

side by side

and the last breath of each and every

long gone soul

living within me

exists my body

today is my last day of mourning

and tomorrow

is the first day

of my very own

brand new story

-regrowth II

brin battisti

nostalgia

the end

nostalgia

brin battisti

brin battisti is a nineteen-year-old poet who has loved writing since she was little. she began writing poetry in March of 2017 and has only grown since then. brin has two other poetry books out. her debut collection is titled 'made of ash' which came out in January of 2019, and her second book followed six months after, with 'things that fall' releasing in June.

she used to swim and dive for her high school, as well as sing in her school's chambers group. she traveled to Italy with chambers to perform concerts. now she studies forensic psychology at the University of New Haven.

you can follow brin on her social media pages below

facebook: brin battisti

pinterest: brin battisti

instagram: @brinbattistipoetry

twitter: @poemsby_bb

tiktok: @brinbattistipoetry

for inquiries, contact brinbattisti@gmail.com

books by brin battisti:

made of ash

things that fall

nostalgia

brin battisti

Made in the USA
Middletown, DE
03 September 2021

47469000R00187